## BOOKS BY EARL SHORRIS

FICTION

Ofay

The Boots of the Virgin

Under the Fifth Sun

NONFICTION

The Death of the Great Spirit

The Oppressed Middle: Scenes from Corporate Life

Jews Without Mercy—A Lament

While Someone Else Is Eating [editor]

PAINTINGS BY
NICK DE ANGELIS

PHOTOGRAPHS BY
SUZANNE
KAUFMAN

# POWER SITS AT ANOTHER TABLE

## AND OTHER OBSERVATIONS ON THE BUSINESS OF POWER

# EARL SHORRIS

A FIRESIDE BOOK
PUBLISHED BY
SIMON & SCHUSTER, INC.,
NEW YORK

Copyright © 1987 by Earl Shorris
All rights reserved including the right of reproduction
in whole or in part in any form
A Fireside Book Published by Simon & Schuster, Inc.
Simon & Schuster Building
Rockefeller Center
1230 Avenue of the Americas
New York, New York 10020
FIRESIDE and colophon are registered trademarks
of Simon & Schuster, Inc.
Designed by Bonni Leon
Manufactured in the
United States of America

10   9   8   7   6   5   4   3   2   1

Library of Congress Cataloging   in Publication Data

Shorris, Earl.
    Power sits at another table and other observations on the business of power.

    "A Fireside book."
    1.  Power (Social sciences)—Quotations, maxims, etc.
I.  Title.
PS3569.H584P6    1986          818'.5402          86-27042
ISBN: 0-671-62293-5

To the members of the
First Monday
Philosophical Society,
with special gratitude
to those who gave
more than they took.

These thoughts
cover thirteen years
during which
the writer lived and
worked
in New York City.
Near the end
of that period,
he suffered two
heart attacks,
which led to some
revisions.

1.

I reject power, but only philosophically, which is to say that I am a liar.

2.

Power is the only pleasure of the day after day;
all other pleasures belong to the moment or the
succession of nights.

3.

Power, like any other dream, is both the act
and the end.

4.

There is no essential difference between great
power and small power; expansion is only a
matter of accessories.

5.

Lord Acton errs: Power is the result of
corruption.

6.

Abdication is the first philosophical act of a
king.

7.

A woman of stubbornness and elegance has the
power to produce a son in her own image; he
has no light of his own. They hold the infinite
arguments of opposing mirrors.

8.

There is no power without arrogance, however subtle.

9.

The power of a man in business is determined by his ability to mask the power of those who dominate him; power is only an appearance.

10.

Power is not relative. Although it shifts, it does not change by degree. Power is or is not; it does not dawn, nor does it leave in twilight. Power is abstract, neither natural nor human.

11.

There are no draws in the games of power.

12.

A Mexican proverb: The rich leave the poor like dishes at an inn, scraped clean and face down.

13.

The weak are destroyed, but not devoured.

14.

A lackey to one man, he is a lackey to his own lackeys.

15.

The president of the company makes jokes about cheating on his expense account to an audience of men who fear they will be caught cheating on their expense accounts.

16.

Men abrogate their lives to their livelihoods.

17.

Upon the announcement of his promotion a party was given by the people who worked for him. They were not highly paid, some did not even earn a living wage. They bought a cake and champagne. It was an expense they could ill afford. He was very moved, surprised, shy. They all laughed together. He understood the solidarity of working people, that rarity. He felt no power over them. He thought: I am now more responsible for them. It would be many years before he understood the meaning of responsibility or power.

18.

People do things for the powerful; they do not wait to be asked.

19.

A powerful man asks for something and is always brought something superior: an urn for a cup, a couch for a chair.

20.

Power is conferred by association: the basking of underlings.

21.

Upon his next promotion there was no party. He had left too many people behind; the distance was too great.

22.

He was upset, at first, by the trappings of power. He sat looking out the window, across the rooftops of the city, all the way to the river. The day was cloudy, hazy. The sun was a pale red spot in the afternoon sky. He looked up at the sun and was shocked at its power to sting his eyes.

23.

Those without power wait.

24.

"I don't want to be a boss", he said. "The only thing worse than having a boss is being a boss." The reference to Lincoln did not go unheeded. He became a boss. "They made me a boss", he said.

25.

Power enables one to break appointments.

26.

In fictions the recourse of the powerless is murder. In life the recourse of the powerless is petty theft.

27.

A man offers me a gift. I have power over him,
unless I accept the gift. I point out indirectly
that it is immoral in business to accept such
gifts, and I do not accept the gift. Now I have
power over him in two areas.

28.

A man who was married to a rich woman still
sought power in business, coming to work in a
limousine to earn his paltry salary.

29.

There is no better way to flaunt one's power than to attempt to appear equal when dealing with the powerless.

30.

When one's power is insecure it is best to remain at home.

31.

Emptiness is a sign of power.

32.

One must achieve power before learning truly
to covet power.

33.

Separation indicates power and power fosters
separation. (Distance may be a better word
than separation.) .

34.

The powerful are made uneasy by deference,
but they accept nothing less.

35.

Underlings speculate about the powerful, but
the powerful discuss underlings in full
knowledge of the situation.

36.

Evil is ascribed to the powerful because they are
unknown; it is the weapon against them.

37.

All power seems evil.

38.

One loses the sense of power over others. To feel power it must be constantly increased.

39.

The wit of power is threatening.

40.

To recognize virtue in an underling is an act of power.

41.

Power is gained by withholding.

42.

The powerful can not enjoy the great cleansing gloom of error; their mistakes are always diffused.

43.

Power is the central position; it is not the
center.


44.

The expression of a complex of ideas, even if it
is incorrect or incoherent, gives one power over
his audience.

45.

Circuitousness is a better means than
confrontation, because it is more certain.

46.

A vision is powerful, unless it is understood.

47.

The most powerful names in intellectual argument are those that are recognized but not known.

48.

Power is embarrassed by unsubtle flattery.

49.

Power is exercised casually; the intense exercise of power is fearsome. The powerful speak slowly, acting as if time were plentiful.

50.

Stylishness, being an acquiescence, mitigates power.

51.

Women covet power, but do not appreciate it.

**52.**

The color of power is dark gray.

53.

Power displays itself in trappings, but names itself by groupings.

54.

The ordinary ring of the telephone indicates nothing. The sign of power is the irritation of the secretary's buzz, indicating that the call takes precedence over the person in the visitor's chair.

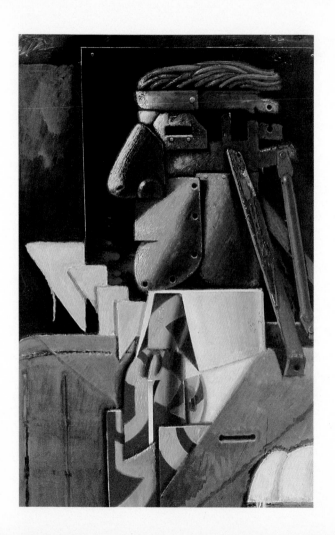

55.

Power has parents and children, but it is
diminished in exact proportion to the number
of its siblings. Fratricide.

56.
The powerful punish by disinterest.

57.
Power always has something of greater
importance.

58.
Parodies are not disrespectful; they are a form
of obeisance.

59.
Power interrupts.

60.
Power expects more, for power satisfied is power wasted.

61.
What had been seen as eccentricity appeared as wisdom after he gained power.

62.

View of a powerful man: If he were not wise,
he would not be powerful.

63.

The powerful are able to cause conjecture.

64.

Clarity vitiates power.

65.

Power lies in wait. The lion need not attack to differentiate itself from the lamb; the possibility of the lion is sufficient.

66.

Power is linear, equality is circular.

67.

Power is impenetrable; thus, the allure of pyramids and doors.

68.

A powerful man never loses control of his eyes.

69.
Noted laughter.

70.
Unpredictability dominates.

71.

Powerful men do not waste their suddenness.

72.

Public defeats, private victories: Only realists can maintain power.

73.

The wisdom of power is to blame the committee.

74.

Power cannot be insulted, although the powerful may be angered.

75.

In modern industrial societies, the relation of money to power is not immediately apparent.

76.

Power is not in making, it is in having.

77.

Conspicuous power is vulnerable.

78.

Indecision cannot be defeated by inferiors.

79.

Envy is a form of obeisance.

80.

All flatterers are lackeys.

81.

Power may be amused, but to be amusing is an admission of weakness.

82.

Power articulates its desires.

83.

Power thanks; nothing more clearly separates the powerful from the powerless than that graciousness.

84.

In the city, power walks; taxis are for those who meet other men's schedules.

85.

Power judges, which is its earned reaction;
strivers initiate, which is all that is open to
them.

86.

A powerful person may choose to send another
in his place; the acceptability of the substitute
depends upon the power of the one who sends
him.

87.

Articulation determines the degree of power, as in the length of a chain.

88.

Power sits at another table.

89.

Only forever is out of reach, unless we define forever as the lifetime of a subordinate.

90.

Love is not power, which may be as good a
description of the human predicament as we are
likely to get.

## 91.
Luck.

92.

Power cringes before the possibility of greater power; the reality is not necessary.

93.

In any contest power begins with the advantage in height and reach.

94.

Power is in no hurry, although someone else is
waiting.

95.

Every act of a powerful person is heightened,
but only in the eyes of the powerless, for power
is always innocent of its own extent.

96.

A powerful man said nothing, and everyone in
attendance knew exactly what he meant. Later,
they could not agree on what they had heard.

97.

Power chooses its dinner companions.

98.

The patience of the powerful.

99.

An entourage precedes.

100.

Reflected glory, but not reflected power.

101.

Philosopher OR king: I have seen powerful
men in the presence of thinking.

102.

Power is negative.

103.

Power attracts; that is the secret of magnetism, and it will remain a secret until clerks become physicists.

104.

Power is arrogated; it always truly belongs to someone else.

105.

There is no power in a small room.

106.

The difference between a powerful man and a bully is the latter's penchant for telephoning underlings at 4:30 on Friday afternoon.

107.
Expertise is a service.


108.
Power abhors a rest.

109.
Invincible generosity.

110.

A man did not know he was powerful; his power slipped away.

111.

The best decoration is a cultured assistant.

112.

It is the divine right of kings to work short hours.

113.

The difference between talking about *money* and *my money*.


114.

A physician's frown.

115.

Powerful businessmen are virile; powerful businesswomen are sterile.

116.

Power does not kill; it permits suicide.

117.

The breakfast hour must not be wasted.

118.

When a powerful man yawns, he expresses boredom; weariness is for the weak.

119.

Power shares intimacy as a reward.

120.

The day of deep voices is long gone.

121.

Complexity is the province of underlings.

122.

Hurried speech is a form of deference.

123.

Power does not advise, it decides.

124.

The measure of power is in the size of its wake.



125.

His family had been wealthy for generations: in him was the explanation for the brevity of the age of kings.

126.

Upon reading Tolstoy's theory of history the powerful man chuckled; later, he announced to his underlings that Tolstoy was correct.

127.

Age stalks power; retirement is the reckoning.

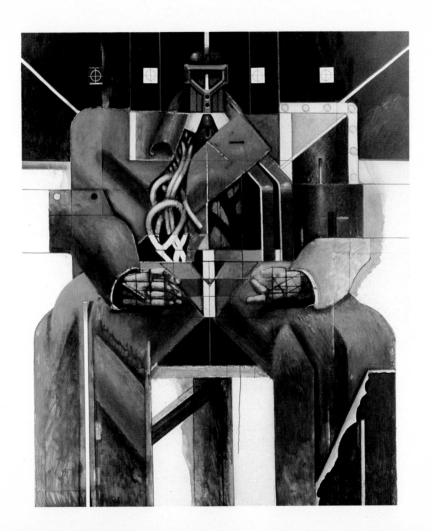

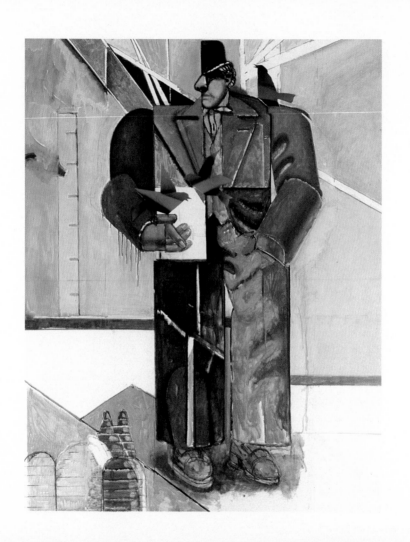

128.

The powerful man kept his options open. He had no use for philosophers, who are immobilized by truth.

129.

An ambitious woman tried to learn to pee while standing up. Her hair fell out.

130.

A powerful woman lived happily with a weak man. One day, she tripped and fell down. He climbed onto her shoulders.

A weak woman lived with a powerful man who grew weaker by the year. She pitied him from an ever-increasing distance.

131.

He knew he was powerful when someone else read the morning paper for him.

132.

Murder has many analogues.

133.

The first step toward getting power is having power.

134.

In ancient Chinese ideographic writing it is impossible to show a king without a kingdom.

135.

Power conserves.

136.

Thought and power can never be congruent.

137.

Force belongs to nations, power to individuals.

138.

To the powerful, art has no meaning, only uses.

139.

A beautiful woman imagined she had power:
She told herself that seduction is a form of
command.

140.

The surface of power is polished stone.

141.

Mere wealth is gelded power, which is why debutantes are vulnerable and attendance at polo matches is poor. Everyone knows.

142.

Speed is the natural defense of power, for power can be lost in contemplation.

143.

The efficacy of power increases with the night.

144.

The range of power: between God and the man with only one enemy.

145.

Power is not an ability.

146.

The power of reason is belated.

147.

Power is not an accident.

148.

A fury of goodness leads somewhere.

149.

Innocence is not a fortress.

## 150.

Power is mortal.

151.

A powerless man inflated himself with aggression. After awhile, he became transparent.

152.

Absolute power lacks duration: A mortal blow.

## 153.

Weakness carps; power crushes.

## 154.

Weakness is known by its given name.

155.

Death has no power, it is dying that we fear;
otherwise, last rites would be said over the
grave.

156.

The test of publicity enforces moral behavior,
according to John Rawls, who has failed to
grasp the power of the big lie.

157.

A man stood before a large audience of subordinates. He began to hyperventilate. In the amassed faces he saw no hostility; they were indifferent. He wondered whether his life itself was an illusion.

158.

This life kneels before the next.

159.

Ultimate power may be safely ignored.

160.

A formula for power: Power equals the weakness of others times their number.

161.

Beneficence is a show of force.

162.

Power cannot be bought, sold or traded, and the bestowal of power must be accompanied by splendid ceremony.

163.

Power is the first compromise of society.

164.

Whenever it is universally known that power is the creation of its victims, the world trembles and becomes the mirror image of itself.

165.

To a starving man a crust of bread is more powerful than a gun—marketing.

166.

Fear of power infects all those who do not despise it.

167.

To be a lackey invites a public execution.

168.

Hell and children derive their power from the same kind of anxiety.

169.

A metaphor: To maintain power one will eventually be required to kill a friend.

170.

During a show of fashions at her most favored lunch place, a woman spread the marrow of her husband on toast, and ate it for an appetizer.

171.

Money is the news.

172.

To choose to tell one's own history is one of the pleasures of power; to be required to do so is to suffer a disaster.

173.

Illness is not power; people attend to the disease, not to the person.

174.

The power of the child over the parent is as basic in the development of the infant as the fear of falling or the urge to suckle; from this illusion of power spring both the will and the imagination to sustain it.

175.

The declension of the power of popular appeal:
Dreck is the past tense of kitsch.

176.

"Do not sit there," my luncheon companion
said, "that is not the power table." A month
later, he had lost his job and could not find
another.

177.

The husband of a shrill and commanding woman visited cheap whores on the hottest and most humid afternoons in hope of contracting a venereal disease.

178.

Delicacy was her only talent. Sometimes, when speaking to her in public, her husband used the most obscene language.

179.

The good humor of despots.

180.

Beauty is to thrall as power is to power.

181.

Power cannot be secured with kindness.

182.

The threat of power is general; power is merely specific.

183.

A dying woman tried to kill her children; she did not want to lose them.

184.

Freedom is the transfer of power from the seller to the buyer.

185.

Age is not a matter of years: One who relinquishes power is old.

186.

In a contest for power, physical strength still plays a major role; there are no neurasthenic titans.

187.

Assumptions keep us awake nights.

188.

A man who did not understand power said he was too busy to attend the company picnic.

189.

The power of an institution gives life to insipid thoughts.

190.

Cities promote one's sense of power, because they protect the ego from the vast scale of nature.

191.

A man relinquished power; reluctance dogged him.

192.

An old man remembered his time of power; in retrospect, in dreams, he was Caesar, Alexander.

An old man remembered his time of power; the importance of it escapes him now.